HELLO GOODBYE

Selected Poems by

Bob Brill

FOR GERTRUDE —
A cherished friend and
a great storyteller

Bob Brill

ZENAGRAF

PRESS

For permission requests, please address:

Zenagraf Press
7300 W Joy Road
Dexter, MI 48130

Cover Art by Bob Brill

Published 2016 by Zenagraf Press
Printed in the United States of America

19 18 17 16 15 1 2 3 4

ISBN 978-0-9627254-3-2

Library of Congress Control Number: 2016911916

For
Barry Spacks
poet, painter, novelist
friend for more than 60 years

and

Laura Lee Hayes,
story teller, writer, gardener,
wife and best friend
for more than 40 years

Preface

At about the age of six or seven I wrote my first poems and stories. I sold my very first story for fifty cents to one of my dad's friends and the guy made off with the only copy. Probably just as well that this story won't surface again.

After graduation from college I knocked around Europe, wrote a novel, came back broke and became a computer programmer to support my habit of eating every day. Wondering why my novel hadn't sold, I reread it, decided to call it a practice novel and relegated it to the landfill. Another story that won't surface to embarrass me.

I married and supported my family as a programmer while devoting my spare time to writing, playing the guitar and composing chess problems. I married again, and upon retirement I wrote several graphics programs and developed my skills as an algorithmic artist. I produced a huge portfolio of math-based artwork, but in late 2003 I set all that aside to focus on achieving my lifelong ambition to be a writer. Now I am devoting my energies to writing fiction and poetry. My novellas, short stories and around 150 poems have appeared in over forty online magazines, print journals, and anthologies.

Occasionally, I'm asked how I get my ideas. Early in the morning, before breakfast or any other activities, I open my journal and start writing without any thoughts or topics in mind. I just keep the pen flowing to let my unconscious mind spout whatever wants to come out. No worries about grammar, spelling, editing or even making sense. A lot of garbage comes pouring out, but often I find jewels floating in the barf. Later I work these up into poems or stories.

Writing is the hardest thing I've ever done, but it is extremely rewarding. I don't write for fame or money. I just like doing it. I get pleasure when I write something I think is good. I also like it when other people enjoy my work, so I have to admit there is an element of vanity in it, but it's the day to day joy of doing the work that sustains me.

My development as a writer has been characterized by an effort to find my own voice and for me that requires more freedom, fewer rules. I began to feel constrained by the conventionally accepted rules of fiction writing as well as tightly structured poetic forms. I started writing more free verse poetry which is less rule bound than rhymed and strictly metered poetry.

I'm very fond of haiku, senryu and tanka, where the tight constraints of those forms taught me how to be concise and shine a narrow concentrated light on a single moment, a lesson that carries over into longer works. Ultimately I needed to break out into longer poems to express more complex ideas.

In the last two years or so I discovered prose poetry, of which there are some representative examples in Section 2 of this book. I find this form extremely liberating for the writer. I still write fiction, but poetry is now my principal focus.

Bob Brill
May 2016

Contents

1: No Words Suffice

Come On, Sadie

Let's dance on the rooftops,
the taxis, the steamboats,
the galloping choo choo trains,
up and down the stairways to paradise.
Let's hop along the stepping stones
across the Milky Way.

Knock the pennies from my eyes.
Take my hand and lift me
high above polluted streets
to a trampoline cloudtop
where the air is fresh
and we can bounce from cloud to cloud.

Let's rinse our brains,
wring them out
and hang them up to dry,
then drift downriver in our little boat
till we get swallowed by the stars
and that big round enchanted butterscotch candy moon.

Comfort Zone

Howling fire trucks and ambulances
rip the fabric of the night.
A few pious souls
offer a quick prayer for those in peril,
while relieved
that it's not happening to them.
The rest of us take no notice.
Turn the page
sip the wine
one no trump
pass the salt
yes touch me there.

Happening Now

Great ocean waves bigger than houses,
ships' flags flap slapping so hard
they tear themselves to shreds

while a woman in Duluth
thinks of her grandmother
as she plants petunias in a windowbox

and a mailman
walking on a street in Cincinnati
thinks of the wife he left in the warm bed.

Tracking a long fly ball heading for his mitt
a center fielder sees a gibbous moon
high in the daylit sky ignoring him.

Clouds shape-shifting as they fly the sky
like giant feathers, like mountains,
like sky-wide shark migrations racing

till the plummeting sun paints them
scarlet orange magenta and a jetliner
draws two pink lines across the sunset

while flight attendants
push their cart along the aisle
offering beverages.

At the bottom of forty thousand feet of darkness
a light winks on in an isolated house
where a man opens a can of tunafish for his supper

and pours himself a beer
as geese pass honking overhead and
distant stars peep through clouds.

Rolling tumbleweeds sweep the desert floor
and the moon scatters its light on the wild ocean chop.
A lone fishing boat rocks on the waves.

All the doings of this moment
like taffy stretching and folding,
peppered with murders and orgasms.

No Words Suffice

Late last night I saw the full moon
spread a carpet of light up my driveway,
turning the garage door into a luminous voice
that whispered of the mystery
that peeps out
thru every crack in the universe.

Now that our celebrated astronauts
have impressed their footprints
in the lunar dust,
cracking jokes and
swinging their golf clubs,
some say the moon has been defiled.

But it will take more than that
to domesticate the moon.
Even the earth,
after centuries of insults
from the bustling human hordes,
still harbors undiscovered secrets.

Some of us humans
like to suspend our quest for riches
long enough to gaze
at the glowing goddess of the night
and glimpse the world
behind the world we know.

Words can describe anything
but fall short of being it.
No words suffice
to express the ineffable
as well as a garage door
swimming in shimmering moonlight.

Blame It On The Moon

At ninety-two
she no longer played tennis.
Dressed in party clothes
she raced her car
toward the rising full moon.

At the funeral
her life was displayed in photos.
An infant in her mama's arms.
An awkward girl of twelve, tall and skinny,
squinting in backyard sunlight.

High school tennis team,
second row, third from the left.
Poised on tiptoe,
ready to deliver a smashing serve
when she was a pro.

Bride and groom cutting the cake.
Posing with her kids holding tennis rackets.
In the last shot her grownup children,
their spouses and kids surround her,
she the only one not smiling.

Her daughter gave the eulogy.
Said her mother never failed
to admire the moon,
a true lunatic
who drove too fast.

Her grandson told his friend
she went and totaled
the Mercedes
that she promised
would one day be mine.

Could be the moon
drew her eyes from the road
as she floored the pedal.
Didn't turn where the road did,
slammed into a tree.

Or maybe she just had enough.
Dressed up to go out in style
and look once more at the moon.
If you can't get the ball over the net,
what's the use of playing?

At the Bottom of the Night

shuttered store fronts
bathed in sputtering neon light
where miniature replicas
of the Statue of Liberty
wait with the endless patience
of the inanimate

in a butcher shop
a single lightbulb
by the freezer door
shows cigarette burns
on dirty aprons
hanging from the meat hooks

heat rises through subway gratings
on a street where the homeless
huddle together for warmth
but for one old woman
who'd rather be cold
than be touched

all is silent
all is still
only the river is moving
the moon sleeps in a cloud
the last bartender
turns out the lights

Null Interlude

nodding over a novel
at 35,000 feet
in the nowhere
between takeoff and landing
between reading and sleeping
between the hero's journey and my own
boarding pass bookmark in the page
where story slips into dream
and the engines propel me
toward my future

I Want a Do-Over

Let me step off the boat in Palma de Mallorca
to discover that it's 1953
and I am 22 years old.
Only this time let me write a better novel,
the one I would write now
had I the energy I then possessed.

Let me be the person I might have been
had I not been blocked
by the person I am.

Let the enormous energy
that went into the waging of two world wars,
and all the wars that came before and since,
be used instead to build a peaceful world
where everyone has enough to eat,
a decent place to sleep,
lots of friends and time to play.

Let the Louis Armstrong Hot Five
be playing tonight at the Michigan Theater
with me in the first row.

Let Duke Ellington and his orchestra
be brought back and given 100 years
to extend the reign
of Duke's musical creativity.

And while I'm at it
can I get the same deal
for Bach, Mozart and John Lennon?

Is all this too much too ask?
Yes, I suppose it is.
We no longer live in the age of miracles,
and perhaps we never have.

Okay, I'll withdraw my request for a do-over
if I can be granted one small favor.
Let me have no regrets.
The life I led was good.
Even when it wasn't,
it was still good.
I just didn't know it at the time.

Empty Bottle Blues

sunlight passing through an empty bottle
casts a green shadow on the wall
such effects are commonplace
yet my skin bristles
as if this time
the universe is telling me a secret

but I don't quite get it
hoping to grasp it more fully
I open another bottle
by the time it's empty
the sun has set
the shadows are gone
an owl is calling
from somewhere in the darkness

Seen from a Footbridge
over the Huron River

Aerial ballet
choreographed by invisible insects
chased by swallows
over the rushing river.

I want to trade my teeming brain
for a pair of swallow's wings.
No one to broker the trade,
so I settle for second best

and fashion the brain I have
into a poet's wand
that captures the living world
in a collecting jar.

Blue wings orange bellies
flashing past my eyes
over the bridge
under the bridge

all around the river
wild curving swallow flight
flattened to a string of words
on a sheet of paper.

Slideshow

In my screen saver slideshow
two colliding galaxies appear.
Slow motion destruction on a cosmic scale.
In the seven seconds that the image remains,
I plunge into a scenario of runaway stars
plowing through vast clouds of hydrogen,
where new stars burst into being
and old civilizations die in fire and ice.

Great temples to unknown gods
vaporize in the inescapable pull of gravity,
and countless eons of exotic cultures,
inspiration for billions of stories
never to be told,
turn into space rubbish.

Could be our own galaxy
twisted in the starry arms
of a grappling sister monster.
Earth slung out of orbit,
all its burgeoning life frozen in darkness,
or swallowed by a rampaging rogue star.
Shakespeare? Not a trace.
Mozart? Not one note.
No one to remember or to mourn,
as though Earth never happened.

As the galaxies fade from my screen,
the next image emerges,

my granddaughter licking a popsicle.
The sun, our good old reliable star,
shines on her face.

As She Sank

This is ALPHA BRAVO FOXTROT ZULU
        ALPHA BRAVO FOXTROT ZULU
   Does anyone read us?
    Our ship is sinking
    If you don't help us
     we're going to drown here

          HOTEL
          ECHO
          LIMA
          PAPA

            UNIFORM
            SIERRA

Notify our families
Pray for us
We came to grief on the icebergs off QUEBEC
We have a bottle of WHISKEY and
the scrapings of an old KILO

This is CHARLIE
Hey I'll tell you of the time
    I got laid in the HOTEL INDIA
    in LIMA Ohio
    the place was deserted
    flies lay dead on the windowsills
    the chambermaid walked in
    while I was drowsing on the bed

I said take off your dress
and she did
after we fucked she told me
her name was JULIET
I said call me ROMEO

MIKE speaking
Last NOVEMBER a potted plant
        fell four stories
        hit PAPA on the back
        he went from doctor to doctor
        they said you're okay now
        look at the XRAY
        he said no I don't feel right
        they said go home
        don't worry
        going down in the elevator
        he threw up a turd and died

VICTOR here
My mother came out of the DELTA country
        walking many days
        before she fell down on the road
        a star descended and spoke to her
        she got up and followed it
        until she reached a GOLF course
        where she fell into the arms
        of a YANKEE merchant
        who became my father

the water is up to our necks
they're living still
in Boston Massachusetts

GOLF
OSCAR
DELTA

GOLF
OSCAR
DELTA

We pray that you receive us
We commend our souls to Thee

        TANGO
        HOTEL
        ECHO
        ECHO

                TANGO
                HOTEL
                ECHO
                ECHO

Birdcage

I love my body
almost as much as I love yours.
Hell, maybe more.

I've had moments
of racquetball perfection,
no thinking, just doing it.

The sex
has been outstanding too.
Sometimes.

I've reached the age
when I have to press my thighs
to rise from a chair.

Whenever I tire of wearing my body,
I long to peel it off
and hang it in the closet,

then take a vacation
where gravity has no dominion
and the bird in me is free to fly.

Out of Body Experience

As if already remembering
I drift out of my body,
away from the woman in my arms
to tell some imaginary listener
how it was in the abandoned now.

How remote she lies behind her shuttered lids,
cool hands that scarcely touch my skin.
Her unbound tresses like a tranquilized Medusa lie
frozen across the pillow,
a river basin from 30,000 feet.

Our bodies are in motion, but who is here
to hold our place in time?
Where is she? Who is she?
This still-life of a lover,
woman with an almost smile.

2: Prose Poems

The Dust Speaks

Where did all this dust come from? What did it used to be or who? Dying flowers falling from the trees. All of us falling away and trampled underfoot. Let time run backward till the dust stands up and speaks. I was Lenny Gold, head crammed with images, memories, ideas, desires, and words by the bushel, by the carload. High on fine Moroccan kief, floating down the wide steps of a moonlit Tangier street all those swiftly moving years ago. I could pull that memory up so clearly, rekindling the airy floaty feeling in my chest mingled with mystery as the street took me curving down into the night shadowed depths of the city, a hide and seek moon following me down. Same moon that shines over New York, so they say, but this was a moon apart, a Tangier only moon that illuminated the merchants sitting on their piles of rugs, smoking their sebsis and sipping mint tea. I had millions of these memories stuffed in my head. But never again will that moon shine. I was Lenny Gold, an obsessive collector of memories. Drinking wine with Darla in our cheap Paris hotel room after hours of romping and rolling in bed, the moon pouring in the window making lovely patterns of light and dark on the curves of her face and body, the rumpled sheets like twisted dunes whose moon-painted flanks were interwoven with a mesh of shadows. A Paris moon transformed our shabby room into an enchanted chiaroscuro engraving. Long afterward my memory would restore her dark eyes, her coal black hair, her beautiful moon-tinted skin. I have been a baby drinking in the world with my mother's milk, a boy blowing up rocks with my chemistry set, a youth full of hormone energy and world-saving ideas, a full grown man riding the wind at the apex of my arc, feeling immortal while knowing I was not, a round shouldered, bent over curmudgeon shaking my fist at the universe when not down on all fours kissing the earth, licking the dust of the king's highway, el camino real, that stretches from can to can't, from yet-to-be to used-to-be, from zip to zot. I was Lenny Gold, all those moonlit memories ago. The wind has blown away my dust.

On On

Lenny Gold took a toke on the pipe. Then a shot of tequila. I need these inputs, he said. Friends, you know me for a ranter who can talk all night. I remember a time years ago ranting in a cheap Paris hotel room till canary jazz warbles in the airshaft told us another day was beginning. Had a picture in my mind that some bed-warm fusty sour-faced Parisian housewife was feeding her canary, the little bird in its cage longing for freedom, the wife too, aching to fly away. All that sorrow dripping from the metro trains speeding people to their jobs, their dentists, their lawyers, their funerals. Darla had gone to bed. The couple we called the Moo Moos were leaning against each other, barely awake. So loving that some of the expats mocked their constant display of affection. Envy is what it was. The only one still wide awake was Tom Weston, who played quiet chords and runs on his guitar, while I kept talking. That was Paris in the long ago.

A demented ambulance, wailing a wild lament as it raced thru the streets, brought Lenny back to the present. He looked at his friends, took another toke and kept talking. It's a million years later and some of us are still walking the planet. Nothing much has changed except everything. The Moo Moos are divorced. Darla moved on, can't say I blamed her, so I had to let her go and move on too. She's forty years older now. We're all forty years older. Can you believe it? On on, there's no where else to go but on on as we're swept thru bottomed out bummers and rocketing highs, speeding on to the next and the next. On on, yet another day, another heartache, another adventure, the death of a loved one, a joyous reunion, a root canal, a fervent lover, a broken ankle. Sunrise, sunset, ghost of a moon shining thru mist, all the beautiful scenery of our lives. Footsteps approaching, receding, people coming and going thru the chambers of my heart. Can't pretend to understand it, but it's so damned interesting. This morning I saw a huge black bird looking at me from a telephone pole. I had to look away. What else can you do but let it all happen? Be here now, be there then, be everywhere there is to be, and submit to the great on on. Pass me that pipe, will you, John?

Your Fingers

You play your flute, a sad Brazilian melody, um samba triste stealing note by note into my heart, your fingers dancing over the keys, making breathy music soar out over the dark water. Your fingers. Your touch tools. You have touched everything with those fingers from squeezing melons in the market to gripping the handlebars of your bike. You've wrapped those long fingers around a pencil and written your grocery list, patted back your long lovely hair. Same fingers holding the greasy corn as you chewed the kernels and licked the corners of your mouth. Same fingers that hold the tennis racket, the towel, the doorknob, the wine glass, ski poles, telephone, steering wheel, teacup, knife, fork, and spoon. I've seen you make a fist, wave goodbye, give the finger to the jerk leering at you from the red sportscar, lick the mayo off your fingers and smile with your eyes as you make sandwiches for our picnic. Your fingers float over the piano keys and a melody flows out behind them, swelling the air. Your clever fingers arranging the cards in your hand, tapping the computer keys, sliding the mouse, advancing a pawn. You touch my face with your fingertips, sending waves of warm feeling thru me. Love fingers. Lady fingers. Long strong fingers that know their way around my body, zipping down my pants, undoing my buttons, reaching under my shirt, smart caressing fingers that find my sensitive places. You press your fingers to my lips. I grasp your hand, kiss each finger and deep in the valleys between your fingers, I lose myself in a frenzy of adoration.

Where All My Comic Books Went

Then I'm stepping out of a movie house in Paris, feeling that momentary disorienting shift as the world of the film dissolves and I reenter the so-called real world, to see hundreds of people running down the street chased by gendarmes wielding billy clubs. I try to get back in the theater, but the attendant locks the door. I bang on the glass. He gives me a no-no sign. I stay under the marquee backed up against the door as far from the street as I can get. I glance at the posters. Coming next week. Gregory Peck in Moby Dick. I hear the sailors singing *Go down, you blood red roses, go down. Oh you pinks and posies.* The ship glides away from the wharf, first moment of the voyage to the great white whale and the bottom of the sea. Up pops a memory of a long lost comic book of Mickey and Minnie Mouse in their cute little open cockpit plane. Black night over the ocean when they run out of gas. Gosh, Minnie, it's been swell knowin' you. They lose altitude rapidly and suddenly their descent is halted, but it's too dark to see what has stopped them. In the next panel the sun is rising over the ocean. You see them sitting in their little plane in the rigging of a sailing ship high above the deck. Saved! But wait. This turns out to be a pirate ship and the nasty pegleg pirate chief has eyes for Minnie. What happened to all my comic books? If only I had known and kept them in mint condition in plastic bags, I'd be a millionaire today. But they are gone where everything goes, where the girl in the green suit went, where Edward went, where we are all going, to that place we call the past which is not a place at all. It's nothing but some spongy gray matter laced with holes and stuffed with frayed memories. The holes grow larger the further the memories recede, till there's nothing left but disconnected fragments, like images in a shattered mirror.

A Poet's Life

Death dances in high heels and here she comes, pounding out flamenco rhythms that punch holes in the floor. I think I've seen this movie. Great special effects, cloaking the story with clouds of churning magic vapor. They make it look easy. Me, I'm still stuck with the noble art of poetry, one lobe tied behind my back and my only tool a tired old bag of words. Yes, it can be done without computer graphics or huge infusions of cash or teams of writers, idea men, cameramen, gaffers, grips, best boys and caterers. The lonely poet high in his tower room with the short stub of a pencil, some scrap paper and a sandwich, turning tuna salad into streams of words. Fluid nonsense dripping down the page. Give us this day our daily quota of word barf, then it's off to the bar to join the other poets who will relish the taste of verses still redolent of tuna. We prop each other up with midnight wit, calling ourselves the Desperado School of Poets. This moment in time, this place on the globe, we're slipping into the same past that all poets, business men, crooks and politicos sink into, even as did the Beat Generation, the Lost Generation, Chaucer and his buddies, the hot young film makers, spreading a mulch on the ghosts of the present, the icons of the past, a whiff of the great times to come and as soon depart. Meanwhile I sit in my tiny garret of a brain pouring out those special effects known as poems, spilling down my legs and pooling on the floor. We were the Desperados, an in group on its way out, fostering each other's illusions, witty and cheerful to the end. Pallbearers of defunct metaphors laid to rest with honors and ironic laughter. I'll write a blurb for your book, old friend, if you'll do the same for me. Not since Virginia Woolf, Thomas Wolfe, and Beowulf has the world of letters seen his like. Thanks, buddy. What else would we be doing? Playing golf? Well, why not? That's just what my cousins do who haven't read a poem since Twinkle Twinkle, Little Star. Golf is as good as any other pastime while waiting for the dancing high heels to deliver the letter bordered in black. Another poet runs out of words.

Words from a Dream

My dreams speak to me, but I've yet to crack the code. Last night's dream dissolved as I awoke. Only two words stayed with me as I opened my eyes in the morning light. Prist and quist. Any meaning they may have had faded with the dream. Plenty of such easy to pronounce strings of letters would serve as good English words, if they could only be given a meaning. If we ever need a word for a spaghetti sauce stain on a clean white shirt we could surely find it among the thousands of letter combinations at our disposal. Perhaps splot would do.

Life goes on in the waking world and it's all good, except that my computer has gone down. Tom has taken it away to his lair, that room with its perpetual Christmas lights and computer equipment where so many nights we've drummed and danced in happy abandon. No emails coming in or going out, no idea whether the stock market is going up, down or sideways. I carry on in joyous ignorance, my heart beating, my lungs sucking up oxygen, my feet tapping to an inner rhythm. Oh the quist of it and the prist of it, whatever that may mean. This is how we lived before computers enslaved us and we managed all right. I'm enjoying this vacation from screen fatigue, viruses, updates, popups, and spam. Today the joys of the slow lane are all mine. With pencil and paper I write in the ancient manual mode. I could happily get used to this and learn to love it, but at the same time, I have an ear cocked for Tom's phone call.

As I stare at the empty space where my computer stood the noise of distant traffic is a constant whispering roar. People out there are commuting from A to B or contrariwise from B to A, each the center of a life, the focal point of an unwritten novel. To write a story one has to carve away 99% of what goes on around us. Let's say the hero walks down the street. The life behind all the shuttered minds is ignored as the hero walks his narrow narrative path to the 7-11, purchase his cigarettes, and make that oh so important phone call to Kitty, while the rest of creation orbits its own joys and sorrows. We could let that teeming multitude be called the quist and the solitary journey of the hero be called the prist. There. Now they are real words with meanings firmly attached. For them to enter the language it remains only that people start using them. I promised myself that I'll say prist or quist whenever it makes sense to do so, maybe even when it doesn't.

Too Many Chickens

Get those chickens out of here, Sergeant. Chickens, sir? Yes, chickens, monkeys, aardvarks, whatever they are, I want them dispersed. Those are not chickens, sir. Those are the men of the 14th platoon securing the perimeter. Whatever they are, they are disturbing my composure. Get rid of them. Yes, sir. And one more thing, Sergeant. I'll have no more of your insubordination. I don't want to be contradicted. See to your duty. Those chickens must go. Yes, sir. The word went down the line. Up the line. It came to the attention of the general that Major Potts was out of his mind. The disease was spreading. Four years in the trenches had taken its toll. The best officers were dead. The rest were pacing in circles, giving senseless orders. The men were ground to their bones, and after numerous advances and retreats, they found themselves in the same trenches as at the start of the war. No end in sight. No way out but death. Bombs were falling from the sky all over the world. The humans had embarked on a mad race to annihilate themselves. The few sane ones were afraid to speak, for those who did were lined up against a wall and turned into hamburger by a stream of angry bullets. Finally the guns fell silent. Sheer exhaustion. The disease had run its course and those who still lived dragged themselves to their feet and looked around at their destroyed world. Slowly the cities were rebuilt. The trees grew back. The flowers bloomed again. Once more humanity resumed its peacetime occupations, the usual crimes, the normal greed, ordinary murder and rape. The economy strengthened, business flourished, new alliances were forged, and the world healed enough for another war to begin.

Long Dead Poets Come to Visit

A party of ancient Chinese poets arrived in a junk to visit the 21st century. They wrote poems of their impressions of our world, noting how so many are tied to schedules, enslaved by their wristwatches, and strangest of all, the emperor had not proclaimed a law that required one to wear a watch. It seemed that everybody wanted one. Even the old Chinese poets took to wearing them, smiling as they showed each other their watches, admiring the ever moving hands, and especially tickled with the slowly rotating arms of Mickey Mouse as the little fellow pointed to the numbers, his white-gloved hands spinning out the hours, minutes, even seconds. The Chinese poets were joined by three 19th century French poets, who renamed themselves Capo, Strabo and Ariago, names they felt were better suited for romantic poets than the bourgeois names their parents had given them. Strabo's poetry consisted entirely of egotistical self display. She was forever looking in her mirror. The two male poets vied with each other for Strabo's affection by writing extravagant poems praising her beauty. Meanwhile Strabo fell madly in love with Wang Ho, who was gratified to learn that the wondrous modern world still embraced this familiar pastime. They rented a rubber raft and went floating down the river wrapped in each other's arms. Capo and Ariago stole a canoe and pursued the love-besotted couple, waving their swords and shouting insults in French. They would have caught the lovers easily if they only knew how to paddle a canoe while brandishing a sword. Oh that Wang Ho, said his friend, Yang Po. He's always been lucky. He got the beauty and the best watch too.

Kingdom of Night

Snow is falling outside my window or inside my dream, maybe both. Numbers are spinning down thru my head and piling up on the floor. Those numbers have dollar signs on them. Gives them a lot more emotional power than mere weather reports or miles per gallon. They're telling me I'm $12,000 short at the bank, making me hyperventilate. More dreams standing in line, waiting their turns. Will I get to see the chief teller before the bank closes, before the flag falls announcing the end of the world? The dice are rattled in the box and tossed out on the table, changing the rules again. One-eyed jacks are wild, aces high. The queen of spades is the spider lady sinking her fangs into my jugular, or is she the angel of mercy offering succor to the weary? It's hard to tell in the winter darkness if the day has begun or it's still the middle of the night when the phantoms of dreams hold sway from their high thrones and legions of orcs and zombies run wild in the streets. The kingdom of night melts away with the dawn and reason once more takes tight rein on the gibbering mind. I pull on my pants, strap on my wristwatch, grab my wallet and appointment calendar. Shlurp coffee to steady the nerves. TV voices offer jolly commentary. Good morning, Hannah, got your head on straight? Your nighttime fears all tucked away till the bloody sun goes down? The market dropped sharply this morning on rumors of world peace. The talks in Brussels are still deadlocked, but a watered-down non-binding agreement is expected to be endorsed, leaving the situation unchanged, if it doesn't take a backward step. A word from our sponsors, the makers of Fukitol, the world's leading brand of tranquilizers. What, me worry? While the sun shines the world grinds on. Newborns leave the hospital by the front door, the dead are taken out the back, jujubes come roaring down the chutes as usual. It's only after the fall of night, when I've got to remove my trousers and crawl into bed again that my mind dissolves in the acid indigestion of insomnia and finally I swim in rivers of sleep, tumbling down the shark infested streams of nightmare alley. The lords of madness plunge my brain in the swirling sewers of dreams where nothing makes sense and morning is a mythical country where my passport is not recognized.

Faster

Fifteen minutes of fame is now down to three microseconds. Only the young, raised on video games, can keep up with this ever shifting post-postmodern world, and they'll oh so soon be watching TV in nursing homes. By the time you get your college degree all your skills are out of date. Sorry, young fella, we don't need no silicon chip engineers. It's all memristors now. The days and nights flicker past in a thrumming gray blur. Came back from vacation to a hundred story condo where my house used to stand. A thousand strangers living there who were born this morning. My wife's a blond now and I've got a mohawk or maybe she's someone else altogether and the same goes for me. The kids grow up overnight and fill these condos while they're still under construction. The wolves are running for their lives. The rabbits are all in experimental labs or Disney petting zoos. We're eating Soylent Green certified organic, makes you sick, but we all have health insurance now. Only way to opt out is to fake illness and kick back at one of the gigantic hospitals till you're done and they flush you down the disposal. Land's too valuable for cemeteries. Buildings so tall you get thirty seconds of giddy weightlessness as the elevator rockets you down to the dimly lit street level where the sunlight struggles to find its way. But then only impoverished losers live down there. The high livers step out of their lofty eyries into their flitters, fly off to the latest rooftop disco, hand the keys to the valet parking attendant, and dance away the night thru the color-coordinated kaleidoscope of the newest designer drugs.

Haiku Magic

I write, therefore I am, and by some miracle of nature, even when I'm not writing, I do not cease to be. I fired a dozen of my haiku thru the e-channel, and now they reside on the computer of the Haiku Society of America, blessed be, and thru the e-channel answer shall return to me. A yea or a nay shall appear upon my screen and I shall cry out yes, yes, yes or oh no, oh no. That's how it's done now. Immaculate connection shall be made and the will of the haiku lords shall be made known. This old world is replete with techno horrors, forsooth, and likewise techno magic to delight the soul. Oh Google, percolating thru the great labyrinth of the world's data. Oh Wikipedia, dispensing words of wisdom and folly on all subjects. Oh Dictionary with its oft consulted Thesaurus, ruling with authority over proper use of our glorious English language. Oh Internet, overarching the world entire. Out of the e-channel spring answers to all questions. What riches I have at my fingertips and by this wand, my trusty mouse, I invoke them. Come unto me oh ye haiku of the ages. By this magic Basho speaks again.

Last Thoughts

What are they waiting for? I'm never going to find out and I don't care. I just want them to get it over with. The captain orders his men to set down their rifles and take a cigarette break. All my life I knew not the hour of my death till now, today, this moment, this is it. Blue sky, clouds slowly drifting, just another ordinary day for these bored soldiers, but not for me. The scent of cedar and cigar dust comes flooding into my mind, my old cigarbox stuffed with memorabilia, baseball cards, movie ticket stubs, coins, marbles, a few odd chess pieces, a Roosevelt campaign button, my old penknife. A black and white photo of a beautiful woman staring beyond the camera. On the back the inscription: Anna 1938. She wears the clothing of 1938. Behind her the sky and clouds of 1938, just like today's sky and clouds. Was she aware of the shadows gathering over Europe, of the monstrous events already unfolding? 1938, me seven years old, sitting on a bench at the corner of Broadway and 91st Street on the wide median strip dividing the uptown side of Broadway from the downtown side, sitting between Aunt Hattie and Aunt Rosie, as I watched the trolleys and cars making their way in both directions, filled with the ghosts of 1938. The trolleys and the tracks are all gone now, even the IRT Subway Station has vanished into the past, the old aunties long ago reduced to faint memories. The soldiers are stamping out their cigarettes. Waking up in the old crumbling stucco-sided Parada Hotel in Miami Beach thinking this is my seventh birthday. We'll go to the beach. Peanut butter and jelly. Anna 1938. Who was she? If I just had more —

3: Hello Goodbye

Rent-a-Poet

Ten thousand voices are screaming
to peel the dollars off your hide.

Kiss nagging back pain goodbye,
but hurry, this offer will expire soon.

Join our crusade to make the world a better place
and we'll send you a handsome tote bag
bearing our logo. Donate Now!

Shut out those voices
and listen to a sweeter tune.
Call Rent-a-Poet.
Invite a real live poet
into your home
to reconnect you
with the beauty of the world.

Of course, my offer can be perceived
as one of the ten thousand voices.
But hey, it's a quid pro quo world
and I've got to eat too.

For a couple of bucks
I'll read you some poems.
I can also mow your lawn
before the dandelions launch their seeds,
or rake your gorgeous leaves
when they drop from the trees,

and in the dark and frigid time of year
when icicles hang from the snow-capped roof
and the snot freezes as it drips from your nose,
I'll shovel the snow off your driveway.

But only if you'll listen to some poems.

City Lights

I ride home in a taxi
after a night of drinking with my buddies.

Theater marquee lights
spinning in endless circles.
I want them to break their chains
and fly into the sky
to form new constellations
that replace the stars we no longer see
behind all the city's lights.

Steam rises from manholes
where workers break open the street
with shuddering jackhammers
drenched in the light of powerful lamps
and the welders' sparking rods of flame.
Down below, dwarves are digging for gold.

A skyscraper under construction rises
into the windy air above Park Avenue.
The night watchman sits in a makeshift hut
drawing smoke into his lungs.
By the fiery glow of his cigarette
I read the story
written in the creases of his face.

An endless river of headlights
passes me going the other way,
while my taxi chases

a long red stream of taillights.
I want to know
who all these rolling riders are.
Where are they going and why?
I scarcely know why I myself
am carried along in this parade.

A million rectangles
of glowing light glide past me.
In a high rise apartment building
I see one solitary window go dark.
Is she lonely as she slides into bed?
I will shinny up the drainpipe to her balcony
and comfort her till it be morrow.

This fantasy is immediately buried
under a slew of fresh impressions
as the taxi rolls past
a new panorama of windows.
To the forgettery with it and everything else
that passes thru my drunken brain tonight.

When I get home I throw up,
turn out the light and go to bed.
I hang on to that rollercoaster bed
as it propels me up Broadway,
city lights careening thru my headache.

Walking

As I hiked a mountain trail in Brazil
beneath the boughs of mighty trees
hung with vines as thick as my arm,
I saw a jetliner far overhead.

So glad to be walking the earth,
my favorite mode of transport,
stopping from time to time
to gaze into the bosom of a flower.

So glad not to be sitting in that plane,
gripping a drink, unable to look
thru my 10-power lens and see
the exquisite vein pattern of an unfamiliar leaf.

Of course, to reach this trail
I had to take a plane
and another
to get back home.

Reflections in the Shards
of a Shattered Mirror

nervous searchlights
slash the wounded sky
burst of pigeon flight and mortar fire

water tower
in slow motion collapse
black smoke drifts across the moon

bullet-punctured rice bags
spill in mud-caked alley
rats hunt thru garbage

bathtub hangs over street
from jagged hole
in pock-marked church

tracer bullets over sagging rooftops
men and boys run with TV sets
thru smashed furniture

bleeding poet
staggers past burning cars
haiku moon in broken glass

blood flows in the gutters
first pink blush of dawn
fading stars

Hello Goodbye

Nothing
big bang
tick tock
everything
stars stars
trillions of stars
a speck called Earth
millions of lives swarming in a dew drop.

Eons later I arrived on the scene,
a Johnny-Come-Lately,
a momentary spark in the great stream of being.
Heart pumping
neurons firing
mitochondria dancing
all systems going non-stop
until the day they do stop.

My hand in yours
your hand in mine
as we hike the rocky road of love
somehow managing
to create the ones
who will replace us
inherit our names
our wealth
and our sorrows.

Dawn stillness.
Distant traffic rumbles thru my dreams.
I roll over in bed and sleep on
till mindless imperious alarm clock screams.
I'm still here
for a while anyway
so I may as well get up.

The sun has not yet ballooned
into a giant star
vaporizing the Earth
and all that it contains.
Not due for another five billion years,
so why do I wake up thinking about it?

We are children of the big bang.
Enfolded in the beginning is the end,
not just you and me
not just the Earth and the stars above
but everything
back to the nothing from which it began.

Brief Encounter

when she walked into the room
her feet barely touched the floor
such grace such beauty
I knew I could spend
the rest of my life adoring her
then she opened her mouth to sing
that was it
over before it ever began

Big Mac

Where the sea wind blows so strong, so cold,
puny boats tossed on wild waves.
Exhausted sailors
with their spindly legs astride the decks,
bringing home gold from the Americas
for their bloody kings.

Fast forward to endless rows of smokestacks
belching noxious fumes,
the price of our ever smarter phones
our bigger burgers.

Such is the world,
forever spinning
its great load of dead.

Gimme Big Mac
double fries
large diet Pepsi.
Gotta have it.
Want it now.

Coming into Denver by Train

in the rocking train
the whistle's throaty wailing cry
as we tunnel through darkness
around the mountain's sloping flanks

the train rounds a curve
to a full moon rising
over the lights of the city
spread out below on the plain

descending by switchbacks
the moon eclipsed and reemerging by turns
as we pass the remaining hills
and hulking dark buildings

we shoot into a narrow channel
of houses close to the track
in the train window
dark houses
lighted windows
flowing past
and the still image of my reflected face
lit by the tiny lamp
over the bed
in my compartment

I catch glimpses
of people in the windows
I see the flickering blue light

of television sets
a man's face
filling a TV screen
talking talking
gone

I picture families seated at dinner
passing the roast around the table
a man in his undershirt
reading a newspaper
feet up on a favorite stool
a boy chewing a pencil
as he does his homework

I imagine a pair of lovers
pressed close together
listening to the wheels
pounding the rails
the rattle of the coaches
and the hoarse moaning
of the whistle
calling the soul
to take to the road
as the train passes
and the uproar fades
the whistle crying faint and far away
they return to themselves
to each other

I pretend to have a magic passport
that would let me enter those fleeing homes
to sit at the dinner table with the family
and listen to their stories
of how they came
to be clustered here
in these houses
by the tracks
on the outskirts of Denver

it would take a dedicated lifetime
to mine this lode
all these lives
that fly past the window
I feel the ache of riches
sifting through my fingers

we roll slowly into Denver station
the great train stops with a jolt
breathing out a soft mechanical sigh
I hear movement and voices in the corridor
as travelers prepare to leave the train

but not I
who still have another two days of travel
before I can reclaim the freedom
to go anywhere I want
on my own two legs
and sleep in my own bed

where sometimes I hear
the distant cry
of train whistles in the night
I heard them as a boy
and wondered what it would be like
to adventure forth into the world

This Page Intentionally Left Blank

Whatever the editor's intentions,
a page is not blank if it contains a message
that the not really blank page was deliberate,
though ineffective as a blank page.

The editor must have had a reason
to let us know that the not quite blank page
was not made blank or nearly blank
as the result of some bizarre accident.

Why this should matter to an editor or anyone else
is a mystery never to be solved,
not because it's so deep or difficult,
but because it's not even worth thinking about.

A totally blank page
would have been preferable
as a space left for doodlers to embellish
while sitting thru a boring lecture.

Or better yet fill the page
with cartoons, crossword puzzles, sudoku,
or my mother's recipe for deep dish apple pie,
or best of all a short poem.

This poem, with its treatise on blank pages,
would fill the space admirably.
I leave the following message for any readers
who feel uncertain about my intentions.

This Page Intentionally Not Left Blank

Bottom of the Ninth

They patched me up,
put me on meds,
and I'm still here.

The me you see
is still me,
but it's late in the game

as darkness descends
over the playing field.
The fans are giving up on the game

and filing out of the bleachers,
ready to go on
to their evening parties.

I'm left here waiting
for my last turn at bat,
hoping that somehow

I can pull myself together
or just get lucky
and hit one out of the park.

In the Peony Garden

The man is bent over his camera
with the huge lens poised
inches from the peony blossom
at the moment of its perfection.

The wind riffles the thin gray hair
that covers his bald spot.
He widens his stance
the better to steady his camera.

He aims to stop time
before the peony drops its petals,
before he can no longer
hold a camera.

Writer's Block

I stagger across
that thirsty desert
with eyes bulging

for a glimpse of an oasis
where words flow in generous
never depleted fountains

and beautiful maidens
serve overflowing cups of metaphors
that spill on the ground of my desire

to spawn a prolific flowering
of words that sprout wings
and fly off in all directions.

Till then I wander the desert
that so resembles
a blank sheet of paper.

The Turtle's Way

"When the wisdom of the Grandmothers is heard, the
world will heal."

— *Native American Prophecy*

He was the captain.
He looked at his watch and his map
saying we will attack then and there.

The wise woman answered
the most you can say is
when? and where?

Her daughter,
the wise woman in training,
said there is also if
and how and what
and why.

But he was the captain
for he was willing
to take the credit and the blame.
As he ordered it, so it happened,
and without knowing the outcome
he determined who lived and who died,
and how it played out
unto the seventh generation and beyond.

The wise women
tended their gardens

and still shared
their wisdom with the captains
who never listened.

In all that time the turtle
lay on a rock in the sun
and when she was ready
slipped into the water
and swam toward her dinner.

Brief Time Out

Rush of endless highway traffic
six lanes all directions
covering a world armored in pavement.
Crowded beaches
sky full of vacation flights
to other crowded beaches.

Fingers entwined
we walk the wavy shifting border
where land meets water,
where day meets night.
The waves wash over our bare feet,
a great comfort
after weeks of stomping
thru snow and slush on city streets.
The last red tip of sun
is swallowed by the sea
and as the sky darkens
the full moon rises over rustling palms.

As we walk toward the hotel,
our toes digging in the sand,
it feels like we're not advancing,
but rolling the great ball of Earth
to make the hotel come to us.

We climb the 403 steps
to the roof of the world
and slip into our hotel room

open to a cool breeze
and the cloak of night
embroidered with stars.

A turbulent flight
that roils the bourbon in my gut
takes us back
to the life we left behind
a mere two weeks ago.

Breaking news from the war zones
canned laughter
unreality shows.
Glowing neon blocks the stars.
HIDEAWAY MOTEL

NO VACANCY

ALL NIGHT PHARMACY

LIQUOR WINE BEER

CHECKS CASHED HERE

Human predators sharpen their claws
as feral children run thru the streets.

Our Beloved Universe

Our universe has stars galore,
more than can be counted.
There must be some life out there
besides bacteria and mosquitoes.
I'm sure there are other planets
that feature love, movies, and flush toilets.

Are there standup comics on far distant worlds?
Are they watching game shows
among the scattered star fields of the Milky Way?
Do they have theme parks in the Andromeda Galaxy?
Or is it all taxes, lawyers, prisons, and homework?

We'll never know the Shakespeare
who lived a billion years ago
in a galaxy at the edge of the universe
that appears in our strongest telescopes
as a tiny speck of light.

I've heard it said
we live in a wondrous universe,
but who knows?
Maybe it's only second rate.
There could be better ones
where peace and plenty prevail
and weekends last for months.

But maybe it's the best universe of all,
especially if it's the only one.

If so, it can't get any better than this,
so there's no point in bitching.
Let's go out for some Chinese food
and celebrate our good fortune.

What the Sea Gives Back

long before there were Wednesdays and Thursdays
before the voice of the lawnmower
was heard in the land
there were long nights of starlight
sunlight filling the tide pools
creatures swarming and dying
waves washing the shore

it's still the same
the tides, the stars
the song of wind and waves

only now you can walk along the beach
and find barnacles clinging to a lightbulb
fragments of bottles made smooth and mysterious
and a green molded plastic toy soldier
aiming his rifle
barely changed by the sea

4: Nothing But Words

Beach Sonata

Starry night on a deserted beach.
No one there to see
a meteor flash across the sky
or hear the incessant murmur of the waves.

Fingers of ocean caress the ankles
of a forgotten beach chair.
Wind riffles the pages of a book.

Dawn light.
Pearl gray waves roll up the beach
to sink into pearl gray sand
and slide back into the sea.

The beach chair lies on its side.
The sea has swallowed the book
and spit it out again
to lie with the other detritus
left along the high tide line.

As the sun climbs the sky,
turning the gray waves green,
the sand a brilliant white,
an elderly woman walks the shore
stooping to pick up shells
to send to her grandchildren.

By noon
umbrellas as far as the eye can see.

Nearly naked bathers jammed together
like factory farm pigs.
Women's bathing caps dotting the seascape.
Body surfing youngsters
scraping their bellies on the sand.
Young men diving head first
into the oncoming waves,
when they're not trying to pick up girls.

After the sun goes down
the families depart.
Time for the lovers
to grapple in the sand
still warm from the sun.

One by one the stars emerge.
When the sand grows cold
and even the lovers have gone,
the beach returns to its primordial state,
except for the lost flip flops,
toys and towels,
abandoned drink cans and condoms,
and the lifeguard's proud imperial throne,
fading in the dark.

Another starry night.
No one to interfere
with the perfect solitude
till dawn and the umbrellas return.

Yellow Sweater

Years ago my mother made for me
a yellow knitted sleeveless sweater.
Yellow was her favorite color.
So cheerful, she said,
this woman whose life was burdened
with a heavy freight of sorrow.

I wore that sweater till I tired
of its unceasing yellow shout
and stored it away
till the day I loaned it to Eva.

The sweater took on a new life,
shaping itself to her feminine form,
displaying as never before
the cheerfulness of yellow.

Eva was obsessed by the dark side of life.
She loved to sing the blues,
dramatizing all their sad and tragic stories.
Her favorite color was a blue
so dark it was almost black,
yet when she wasn't singing,
she was irrepressibly bouncy and cheerful.

It was clear that Eva fancied me.
I could have had her in a heartbeat,
but my heart was beating for someone else.
I was frantically pursuing Allison

of the green eyes, the red sportscar,
and the sexy black stockings.

I spent four months
in a crowded orbit around Allison,
till she announced her engagement
to a rich lawyer.
We disappointed suitors dispersed
to try our luck elsewhere.

I felt that I had escaped
from a whirling salad spinner,
still somewhat disoriented,
but free at last to resume my life.

My thoughts turned to Eva,
but she was no longer waiting for me.
She had accepted an offer
to join a blues band in Austin, Texas.
When she came to say goodbye,
she was wearing my yellow sweater
and her signature dark blue scarf.

I did not ask her to return my sweater,
nor did she mention it.
Goodbye Eva.
Goodbye yellow sweater.

Where the Impossible is Ordinary

No need to pack a bag.
Just shut your eyes and wait
for the dream master
to wrap you in her dark glowing cloak
and project her movies in your head.

Where your beloved dead visit
for conversation and adventures,
and you wake up thinking
you have missed an opportunity
to find out what's going on with them now.

Where the dream story is so sweet
that you never want to wake up
and lose that beauty
beyond all back-scratching bliss,
but you come awake and it's gone.

Where you take such fright
that suddenly you're wide awake,
sitting up in bed with horripilating skin.
You refuse to go back to sleep,
but you do.

There's more in that nutshell
than can be grasped
with our greedy claws
and brought back undamaged
to the quotidian plane.

Nothing But Words

A breaking wave made entirely of words
races up the beach to deposit its load of debris.
I search the tideline for any striking new words.
Among the usual words like seaweed and starfish
I spy an exquisite gem, *haberdashery*.
Only the tip of the tail of the y is broken off.

I find another rare beauty,
the word *jejune* lying on an unbroken moon shell.
Such words sometimes emerge
from the great treasure house of the sea.
How they get there no one knows.
Perhaps they fall overboard from a passing poem.

Two choice specimens in one day
tucked into my collection bag
and carried home to hang
with the others on the wall.
My house is made of words
like windows, doors, roof and chimney.

The walls are not made of bricks,
but of the word brick repeated in neat rows.
I myself am a skin-covered bag of words.
When my brain fills up with poetry
I spew out verse like rolling dice
across a sheet of paper.

Après Nous

in a junk-filled yard
a rusted car on cinder blocks
no tires no doors
through the round hole in a fender
where once a headlight gleamed
a sunflower opens its petals

Deneb

a beam of starlight
three thousand years
on its journey
reaches Earth just in time
to pass through a momentary hole
in the cloud cover
penetrate my eyeballs
unleash cascades of neurons
and trigger the manifold circuits of wonder

other clouds move in
and snuff out great Deneb
but a few million neurons
still zing around my brain
finally to extrude a poem

Bird on a Bike

Every morning the old guy has coffee
and a walnut scone at the same sidewalk café,
sits in the same seat
at the same table
where he can watch the world go by
at the intersection of two busy streets.
It pleases him
to have a front row seat
at a spectacle he can observe
without participating.

Today he is annoyed to find
that someone else has taken possession
of his table, a couple who are laughing
and clinking their coffee cups,
wearing jog pants
with white stripes down the legs.

And what is worse
a new waiter takes his order.
Maurice never had to ask.
He just brought the café au lait and the scone.

A group of sparrows are pecking
at the crumbs around his customary table.
They always do, but seen now from a distance,
at a different angle, it's a different world.

Behind the couple two bicycles are parked,
leaning on their kickstands side by side.
A sparrow lands on one of the bicycle seats,
jauntily perched, looks around,
hops up to the handlebars,
pauses a moment, takes wing
and is gone.

The old guy smiles.
This is no caged bird constrained
to keep returning to the same perch.
This bird is an improviser,
free to park
on whatever perch is handy,
then off to the next adventure.

The old guy calls over the waiter.
Please put a shot of rum in my coffee.
A week later he's snorkeling
in the lagoon of Bora Bora.

Show Biz

Give the little lady a big hand.
She's doing her best to entertain you,
doing the splits
and showing her tits.

Never mind that one fine day
in an unanticipated future
she'll need a hip replacement.

Her loyal followers,
who buy her dinners
that start with wonton soup
and end with fortune cookies,
will all be gone to their several destinies
with troubles of their own,
so nobody will gallantly step forward
to pay her hospital bills.

She'll have her dear little kitten
to curl up in bed with her,
and she'll comfort herself
with mystery novels and chocolates
and the occasional breakfast in Harlem.

Just another copyrighted drama
of life among the little people
who hold up the great pyramid
where the elite gather
in their penthouse condos

to bitch about their boredom
and curl up in bed with
their faithful kittens.

Taxi! cries the little lady
with the prosthetic hip,
take me to the LaLa Club
where the in-crowd goes,
where the waiters know them by name
and give them the best tables
close to the dance floor.

The show girls here
don't do the splits,
don't show their tits,
never need surgery,
never grow old.

Breaking News

shouting voices
3 a.m.
door slam gunshot
neighbors friends
cops reporters
high-speed presses
morning extra
latest news on
breakfast table
coffee stain on
victim's photo
paper tossed in
garbage can
next edition
screaming headline
seven dead in
tenement fire

Not Now

I embrace her
to offer support
in her time of grief.

The warmth of her body
heats the desire
I didn't know I had.

I press her close,
she kisses my cheek
as tears stream from her eyes.

This is not the time,
not the place,
maybe not even a good idea.

We separate,
but a signal has been passed
that will be processed at a later time.

It Is What It Is

I close my eyes
and watch
gulls rise from fog
to circle
above the rockbound coast
of my imagination.
I hear their cries,
the rush of water up the beach,
the hiss of retreating waves
sinking into sand.

I open my eyes
and I'm still here
where I was before,
in a pale green room
in a cheap hotel.
Sunlight filters through dirty panes,
illuminating gently floating dust motes.
A light breeze stirs the curtains,
ever so slightly modulating
the play of light.

So consistent,
the way it seems to illustrate
the laws of nature
as in a physics textbook.
So beautiful.
So frightening.
The iron laws at work,

grinding out the moments of our lives.

Behind the fluttering curtains
in this cheap hotel,
an unthinkable energy dance,
a roily boiling flux.

The universe itself
may be a dust mote
floating in a sunbeam
inside a pale green room
with fluttering curtains
in some cheap hotel
in another universe.

There is no strange.
There is no normal.
It is what it is.

I make myself focus
on so-called
everyday things,
like fifty feet of coiled garden hose,
a pile of mail in a wicker basket,
a lump of butter
melting in a frying pan,
a vase of red roses on a table,
a truck grinding into low gear
as it turns a corner.

We own the words,
shooting them like bullets
till we feel that we are
who we say we are,
that there are such things
as the words describe.

Pass the salt, please.
I've got to catch an early train today.
I read in the paper that a new building
is going up in the financial district
that will be taller than the Peanut Butter Building.

Such talk steadies the world,
stops it from spinning,
so we can stand
without getting dizzy
and walk around
like we own the planet.
So the sun can arc across the sky,
and the carousel of stars come wheeling after,
while the earth remains solid,
stable,
and flat,
and the Nasdaq rises and falls
of its own sweet will.

Photons, protons, quarks.
Mere words,
handles to grasp the ineffable.
Just as fictive
as seagulls coasting through my mind
or a vase of red roses on a table
or fluttering curtains
in a pale green room
in a cheap hotel.

Without a Trace

Oily aliens gather for annual mating ritual,
rubbing antennae with their neighbors,
sex in a pile of bodies.

Their wobbly star goes nova.
Mating ritual vaporized in mid orgasmic throb.
No alien poets left to compose the final epic.

We'll never get to read their poetry
and we wouldn't understand it
even if a collection of their poems

turned up in The Library of Congress.
Would we observe a minute of silence
to call to mind the loss of their world?

Not a chance.
We don't even know that they existed,
much less disappeared.

Besides, it's just a fantasy
that was spawned in my back brain
during a power outage on a stormy night,

but I wonder will it matter to anyone
among the distant starfields
when it's our turn to vanish?

Two Portraits

he came in slamming the door behind him
saying oops
but I noticed his smile grow larger
this slambuoyant friend of mine

doctor told him
you have a pathological condition
how true said my friend
I walk the path illogical
leaping off high cliffs
at least two feet tall
falling on my face again and again
but it's worth it
for the times I land on my feet
astonishing everyone

he jumped out of a plane in his undershorts
in harness with a half-naked woman
contrary to some people's expectations
(or was it their secret wish?)
the chute opened and they landed safely
laughing and shouting and rolling on the ground

bittersweet the mixture
of admiration resentment and envy
as I said well done asshole
you should try it sometime he said
to me who always plays it safe

Low Battery

Full body Xray scan
at security checkpoint
stripped me more than naked.

Inhaling the heavy atmosphere
of airport anxiety
was like breathing glue.

The airport prologue done at last,
the plane screamed down the runway
and clawed its way into the air.

A boring magazine with salty peanuts,
a shot of booze, a little snooze,
and another airport rose up to meet us,

looking like the airport I left behind,
same baggage carousel
with nearly identical black bags.

My taxi darted into the street
before my door was closed.
The twitchy driver honked his way

thru snarling traffic to my hotel,
exact duplicate of the one last year,
a thousand miles ago.

In the casino
a hooker tried to snag
a piece of my luck.

When my luck turned sour
she went looking
for better game.

Home again,
had no fun,
met no one I liked,

but I did resolve
the uncertainty that bugged me:
I didn't get the job.

Woke up this morning,
checked my vital signs.
Another low battery day.

Went back to sleep
till late afternoon
when hunger got me up.

Found two hardboiled eggs,
not very fresh, but hey,
felt lucky to have them.

I live in a world where
lottery tickets litter the floor
and empty wine bottles fill the trash.

No Can Do

she stands on the cliff
bare toes curled over the edge
crouched to spring
arms raised for flight
just as she begins to feel
the acid coming on

she keeps telling herself
there's nothing I can't do
but just in time
she remembers
she is no bird
no wings
no feathers
no flying lessons
no pilot's license

straightening up
she steps back
still gazing at the sky
where pearly clouds float
and an eagle rides the thermals
she sighs and turns away

looking down at her feet
she walks back to her car
too stoned to drive

Nature Study

an insect
barely visible
like a tiny metallic jewel
pauses
on the rim of the glass
if I'm quick
I can whip out my 10-power lens
and see the exquisite detail in its wings
before I accidentally knock it into the orange juice
and it drowns

So Begins My Wander Year

with a deep throaty whistle
the ship shudders into motion
my wild heart
echoes the throbbing engines
I stand at the rail
and watch my parents
melt into the waving crowd
that dwindles to nothing
as the shore slips away
into the past

5: Poets of the Far Future

Florida Suite

dusk in the lagoon
a heron fishing
fades in the thickening dark

sand pail and shovel
beach chair overturned
cloth rippling in the wind

behind the beach hotel
screened by oleanders
two boys smoking pot

in the lobby
surrounded by luggage
a woman scolding her child

a well dressed man checks in
with a woman and no luggage
slides a fifty to the desk clerk

in the cocktail lounge
a woman drinks alone
men at the bar staring

the band leader
at a white piano
happy smile pasted on

in a third floor room
an old man gasping for air
distant rumba, cha cha cha

in the room next door
a couple dressing for dinner
argue about money

the night clerk is late
the newly married day clerk
keeps checking the clock

on the front porch
women sharing stories
photos of grandchildren

men playing pinochle
recall the old days
horses women the war

young men without dates
their boisterous shouts and cries
rushing them along the sidewalk

in the street
whispering tires
on wet pavement

night in the lagoon
fish swimming
through black water

The Black Watch Cap

somebody stood
at the foot of her bed
wearing a black watch cap

I'm going to take you
where the rough sailors dance
in their black watch caps

they will devour you
with eyes with hands
in their black watch caps

they will pass you
from man to man
in their black watch caps

he chased her through
the endless halls of sleep
in his black watch cap

exhausted she woke alone -
on her pillow
lay a black watch cap

Autumn Song

falling leaves pile up in the gutters
mounds of treasure lining the public way
leading our eyes down stately aisles of splendor
such abundance of beauty
that we have to sweep it up
and cart it out of our way

Beach Shack Escape

Too many people,
too many cars, lawnmowers and leaf blowers.
I escape to an island deep in my mind
where I live in a ramshackle beach shack
and sit on the porch in a wicker chair,
strumming a guitar.

Yeah,
I like that fantasy,
but if I try to drag my dreams into reality,
it never works out as intended.
The beach is great,
but the food is terrible,
and the landlord
keeps bugging me for the rent,
even though I paid three months in advance,
plus the shack has no screens.
Mosquitoes the size of battleships.

Two police persons stopped me
as I walked along with my groceries,
a six-pack and a jar of pickled herring,
to ask if I saw
a red Ford Escape speeding past me.

No sir, I didn't notice any cars.
I was looking up at the palm trees,
inventing a little story about
monkeys throwing coconuts at each other

till one excited monkey
forgets to let go of his coconut
and finds himself flying
head first into a tree.

We're taking you down to the station
to book you for careless daydreaming.

Wait a minute. This daydreaming
is a vital component of my poet's toolbox.
It slides me into a charmed head space,
sometimes, I admit,
even as I'm crossing the road.
I could be run over by a red Ford Escape
fleeing a murder scene
while chased by a pack of coyotes
trying to rescue a kidnapped duck.

Get in the car.
You're a menace to traffic.

Good thing all this is happening in my head.
There are still too many people
and too many cars,
so I spend more time in my beach shack
now that I've got screens in the windows.

Poets of the Far Future

1

After the extinction of the humans
a few million years may go by

before the voracious roots and suckers
of the immortal vegetables

will erase our highways and parking lots,
leaving only rusted metal junk

and shards of everlasting plastic
festooned with foliage.

Even our graves and landfills
will dissolve into mush.

Giant birds will roost
on the vine-covered skeletons of skyscrapers.

2

Big brains will climb again
to the top of the food chain.

Perhaps they'll be almost human.
I picture them with tails

and a third eye
to foster empathy.

Alchemists of the far future
will discover gunpowder.

Only a few centuries of experiments
before they'll invent the hydrogen bomb.

Historians of the far future
will offer some groundless speculation

about their predecessors,
who they were and where they went

without knowing a thing about
our mad glorious tragic history

or what they could have learned
from our mistakes.

3

Poets of the far future
will reinvent all the tropes and styles

of the long extinguished human poets.
Some will celebrate the exploits

of latter-day warriors and kings
without ever having read the Iliad.

Some will sit in rusted cars
playing with the steering wheel

and write odes to the mysterious beings
who left their trash behind

when they sailed away
in their sky chariots.

At least one, copied by
a whole school of poets,

will get drunk
and drift downriver in a rowboat

while looking up at the moon
without ever having heard of Li Po.

And that same moon
that enchanted the ancient poets

will have moved into a lower orbit,
will loom larger, create higher tides

and wield greater power
over the moon-addicted drunken poets,

who alone of their tribe
will foresee their successors

marching again down the same path
in a beautiful moonlit world

where the sun will go on shining
until it doesn't.

The Janus Effect

I pull up memories
or at best their tattered ghosts
even while rushing

into a hypothetical future,
trying to make it
all come out in my favor.

One eye looking back, one eye peering ahead
and a third eye trying to shut the Janus eyes
and live in the moment.

Sometimes so much happens in that moment
that it feels like a week.
Going to a funeral,

surviving a train wreck,
and winning a hundred bucks at poker
all in one day.

Sometimes the time machine slows down
to an inch worm's pace
as I wait impatiently

for something to happen.
She's ten minutes late.
Is she going to stand me up?

Come on, come on,
show up already
or the movie will start without us.

If only I had brought a book.
I'd have something to do
while waiting for time to get unstuck.

Ah, there she is, sweet thing,
hurrying toward me with excuses at the ready.
This will slide away into the past.

Ten years from now will I remember
the movie we saw and
where we went for dinner?

The waiter with the Danish accent?
The candlelight? What wine we drank?
Kissing in a taxi?

Forty years down the road
will I remember what's-her-name
and the guy she married?

The Janus eyes have cataracts,
squinting at a blurry past,
altogether blind to the future.

Dream Writer

I dreamed I was reading a novel by Martin Amis,
went something like this:

I received this six-pack day a missive
shot like an arrow in the spleen
whose pungent phrases
goaded me to reinhabit
a stoned throw away
that filth-spattered flat
where late I loitered
awash in empty bottles
and teeth-gnashing arguments,
and where the termagant I escaped
still resides. God love her.
I can do so no longer.

Coming slowly awake in the dark
I realized the words
were not Martin Amis's but my own.
My dream, my words.

I lay in bed
morphing that phrase
a stoned throw away.

Could have been a stoned throwaway,
reminding me of a wedding ring
my wife found in the Grand Canyon.
Someone might have

flung that ring from the canyon rim
in an altered state of mind.

Or a throned stowaway,
evoking a royal personage
fleeing a purge.

Night time thoughts
stirring the cauldron of poetic gravy,
when words can go slip sliding around
like dice in the dice box,
rice in the spicebox,
mice in the icebox.

If I could fully access my dreams
I would let that inspired dreamer
compose my poems.

Pete's Last Ride

one time
one time only
a motorcycle was her chair
that chair flying
down a long straight country road

young Pete driving
she hanging on behind
her arms about him
one hand in his pants

no floor
but the streaming road
below their feet
no walls
but the whistling wind
no roof
but the overarching trees
whip whipping past

Pete's strong body
Pete's steady grip

a sudden turn
made her gasp
as he left the road
plunged onto a narrow winding trail
through a sumac thicket
braked to a stop

he took her hand
led her from the bike
tumbled her
in the grass
by a field
with corn
just breaking
the earth

two weeks later
cold spring rainy night
Pete sprawled under his cycle
head against the curb
on wet city street
painted with bright
stabbing
headlights
taillights trailing long red smears

ambulance roaring to a stop
medics bending down to
lift the bike
from Pete's twisted body
could not make out the words
that bubbled
through the blood
oozing
from his mouth

Becoming

Age 15, me,
virgin masturbator with a chemistry set.
The pictures of airplanes
that adorned my bedroom walls
gave way to photos of scantily clad movie stars
who displayed the mysteries of cleavage.

Looking out my window
on the 2nd floor of our suburban home,
I first saw Orion
rise majestically on winter nights.
Thru this window I learned the Pleiades,
Capella, Aldebaran, Castor and Pollux.

One morning I looked down
to see a little girl
age 4 maybe 5
playing on the sidewalk
in front of the house.
I could see from her movements
that she was inventing a game,
pretending to be a grownup,
perhaps the queen of England
parading before her subjects.

She will outlive me
was the thought that flashed thru my mind.

Now 70 years later,
when the mysteries of cleavage
had long been resolved,
I think of that child.
She could be a grandmother
watching her children's children
growing toward grandmotherhood.

She could be a blind woman
sweeping her cane before her
or a homeless bag lady.
She could be an aging movie star
with cleavage of her own.

She may appear so ordinary
that no one would notice her on the street.

She could be lying in her grave.

Moment by moment we grow
into the next instar of our being,
so that after a billion heartbeats or so
what we have created is a life.

Yet Another Dream

The rain had stopped.
The streets were wet and
Gli Burn and I were walking
through the hot night air.

We looked up and saw
the open star cluster
known as the 40,000 Horsemen
melting and sliding down the sky.

The dripping stars landed
ten yards ahead of us
with a soft plop and made
tiny splashes on the wet pavement.

In a lovely end of the world mood
we walked on in silence,
drinking in the delicious atmosphere
of desolation and loss.

This was shattered
when an ice cream truck came by
playing Mozart's Dishmop Serenade
on its tinkly calliope.

Far away a howling fire truck intruded
and the dream began to unravel.
I kept my eyes shut
but it was no use.

The wet city streets were gone
and with them Gli Burn,
the ice cream truck,
the melted stars.

I told Gli Burn he would have to be strong
to pass into the quotidian plane,
but he was just a dream person
and preferred to stay where he was.

The fire truck dopplered away,
a real world fire truck
on the way to a real world fire
or an emergency cat rescue.

I was left alone to prepare
for another day at the office
enduring boredom for a paycheck
on an ordinary Thursday morning.

The Lost Traveler

Gluten glaben fluten flaben
Wait, I fix this. Gimme a sec wudja?
There, I've adjusted my translator
to speak your luvly American tunguage.
You read me okay?
My words they maken sense?

Yeah, okay, good,
so here's my questiown:
where am I?
What I mean,
where in relation to my home planet.
You dig?
I wanna go home.

I so lost,
turned into wrong spiral arm,
not even sure this is right galaxy.
Your planet got a name?
Your star wot's it called?

My star called Gluten.
You never heard of it?
If I knew how to get there from here,
I wud go home tootsweet
and you wud see me no more,
not even once more.
I mean never more.

I looked around at these strange creatures
and thought of my beautiful friends.
Among my own kind I am considered good looking,
but folks here think I'm weird.
In truth they are the weirdos.
Imagine: only two eyes, two arms, two legs.

A small person,
just a boychik, I was told,
followed me around.
He said no way (quaint expression)
can we find your home
and even if we could,
we have no way (again no way) to get there,
so you'll have to live here with us.

He walked around me to observe
my 3 eyes in front, 2 in back.
Peculiar, sez he.
Me talking, how do you make do with no eyes in back
to prevent someone stabbing you with a pelákasar?
I see your point, sez he.
Yes, those pelákasars, sez me, have sharp points.

We became friends when he showed me his yoyo.
Good tricks he taught me.
Skin the Cat (whatever that means).
Rock the Baby, not easy, but I learned it.
They're gonna luv it when I show them at home,

if I ever see home again,
the probability of which is close to zero.

Then I popped the kid's eyes open
doing six-handed yoyo,
three different tricks at once.
He made me do a yoyo show for the whole village.
That's when his people accepted me.
I can chop wood and milk cows, all at the same time,
and keep a yoyo spinning too.

I miss my wives.
The females here are too alien for my taste.
The food is not great, but it keeps me going.
I do like spaghetti.
I slurp it up, one strand at a time.
No one else eats it that way,
but they don't mind if I do.

To Benton at Age 5 Months

I envy you babies who bathe all day
in the shimmering golden light
that streams through the nursery windows.
You have yet to learn the ropes
that tie us in knots
and choke off access
to the infinite bounty
of the suck-titty world.

To the Goddess

You cup the moon in your palms,
the earth in your belly.
You send down the rain
that brings forth the harvest.

Tonight,
while we still crawl across the backside of time,
the sheriff's hounds are loosed and lusting
for the smell of your garment.

When your time comes round again,
you will transform the junkyard
with blossom and birdsong.
The sheriff and his deputies
will bow down before you.

The moon
looks down on your hiding place,
waiting thru the bitter years
for your return.

It Is Always Now

I am sitting at my desk
writing with a ballpoint pen
to the generations yet unborn
or now in the bud preparing to open

you will know the rain
you will know the moon
the tree and the stone
the same sun that shines on me
the same fire that consumes the candle
the rose that opens its petals
that drops its petals
you will suck the oyster from its shell

as you read this you will see me
with my ballpoint pen poised over the paper
even though I will be gone

As I was writing in my journal one morning, I did not notice my wife, Laura Lee, sticking her head in my room and taking this picture. When I heard the click of the camera, I looked up and had to laugh. She calls this picture *Poet at Work*.

Photo by Laura Lee Hayes

Acknowledgments

Many of the poems in this book were published in the ezines, print journals and anthologies listed below.

A Handful of Dust, Apeiron Review, Aphelion, Curio Poetry, Diverse Voices Quarterly, Magnapoets, Of Sun And Sand (beach anthology), Peninsula Poets, Petals in the Pan (flowers anthology), Poetry Pacific, Pyrokinection, Red Fez, Storm Cycle 2015 (The Best of Kind of a Hurricane Press anthology), The Battered Suitcase, Water Music: The Great Lakes State Poetry Anthology, Wilderness House Literary Review, Willows Wept Review, Underground Voices.

Thanks to Jerry Friends and his staff at Thomson-Shore for their skills in book production and distribution.

Thanks to Laura Lee Hayes for extremely valuable help with every stage of producing this book.